Strengths in the Workplace

Harnessing Character Strengths for Success

Copyright © Jeremy P Farrell 2023

All rights reserved. No part of this publication may be reproduced, stored in a retrieval system, or transmitted in any form or by any means without the prior written permission of the publisher, nor be otherwise circulated in any form of binding or cover other than that in which it is published and without a similar condition being imposed on the subsequent purchaser.

The right of Jeremy P Farrell to be identified as the author of this work has been asserted by him following the Copyright, Designs and Patents Act 1988.

www.thegrowthlab.org

authors@thegrowthlab.org

jp@jpfarrell.co.uk

www.growthlab.pro.viasurvey.org

Other books in the series:

Create a Resilient Project Management and Delivery Culture

Moving Back to the Future

The 4 Steps of Powerful Coaching

Contents

Foreword 9

Chapter 1: Positive psychology, productivity, meaning and purpose 13

    Strengths 13

    Happiness 15

    Character Strengths 17

    Real stories 19

Chapter 2: Character Strengths 21

    Horsepower 22

    Wisdom and Knowledge 25

    Courage 27

    Humanity 29

    Justice 31

    Temperance 33

    Transcendence 35

Chapter 3: Character Flaws 37

    I am better than you. 39

    I am worse than you. 39

    I deserve what you have. 40

    I do not deserve what you have. 40

    Strength of character and character strengths 43

Chapter 4: Clifton's Strengths 45

    The 34 Clifton Strengths: 48

    Executing: 51

    Influencing: 53

Relationship Building: 55

Strategic Thinking: 57

Chapter 5: Mapping VIA Character Strengths 59

Mapping to Flourishing PERMA 61

Mapping Character strengths to MBTI 62

Mapping Clifton's and the Character Strengths 63

The VIA Character Coefficient 64

Mapping Talent Themes 65

Mapping Character Strengths 66

Chapter 6: Personal Development 69

Flow 71

Your character strengths 73

A strengths-based career path 75

Your signature strengths in the workplace 77

Chapter 7: Strengths in the workplace 79

Creating a strengths-based workplace culture 82

Identifying character strengths in job candidates 84

Leadership in a strengths-based culture 85

You take your character with you 87

Chapter 8: Leveraging Strengths for Teamwork 89

How teamwork and strengths are related: 91

Individual strengths in a team 93

Building a strengths-based team culture 95

Coaching for motivation and improvement 97

Chapter 9: Harnessing and Developing Character Strengths 99

Appreciation of Beauty and Excellence 100

Bravery 101

Citizenship 102

Creativity 103

Curiosity... 104

Fairness 105

Forgiveness... 106

Gratitude 107

Honesty 108

Hope 109

Humility 110

Humour 111

Kindness 112

Leadership 113

Love 114

Love of Learning 115

Open-mindedness 116

Perspective 117

Perseverance 118

Prudence 119

Self-Regulation 120

Social Intelligence.. 121

Spirituality 122

Teamwork... 123

Zest... 124

Conclusion: 125

Appendix 127

Organizations using strengths for success...........................129

Foreword

What do you enjoy about reading? More specifically, what do you enjoy about reading novels?

Regardless of the genre - Sci-fi, romance, drama, crime, espionage -we read book after book because they inevitably take us into the protagonist's world and life challenges. We read because we get to know someone new, their values, personality, talents and character. As we get to know them, we learn to love or loathe, respect or disrespect them, defend or criticize them, and become involved in their story.

Fictional characters need to have a back story. When they do not, they have no depth, and we get bored with them. The successful author introduces you to the character, what they value, what influenced them, what hurt them, what excites them, and how they act under pressure. We need to know whether to boo and hiss as in the pantomime or to cheer as we do for the athlete.

A successful story draws us into the life of some key characters and ultimately invites us into the world of convictions and principles of one person. Our characters have personalities, talents, aptitudes, tastes, disabilities, intellect, physiology, faith, belief and confidence. They are people with all the good and bad we can demonstrate- so we are led to identify with someone in the story.

A typical formula of fiction is the 'three-act play'. A succession of problems requires the hero to make value choices to overcome them. The third of these problems is a crisis that poses the most significant test of character. Will the hero take the easy way out and compromise their values to resolve the crisis, or will she make the tough stand, the more challenging path, that achieves resolution without compromise? Will she show the depth of character? Will she make us proud or disappointed? Will she rest in peace (dead or alive) at the end of the story, or suffer the torment of knowing she sold out? Will you want to read another book with her as the protagonist?

The finest authors create the worlds in which our characters live. They paint us pictures in oils and pastels, in charcoals and ink. They give life to those worlds with smells, sounds, textures, machines, and structures. They take us into a new country, time, culture, religion, war or debate. We love this immersion into the new, the different. But without characters with whom we identify or aspire to be, these are travelogues and documentaries.

We are drawn to the depth of character. We are drawn to characters who consistently live out their positive values in good times and bad. We find parts of ourselves, heroes and heroines, strengths and flaws in them.

In memoirs and biography, we read to share the subject's life journey, to understand why they did what they did, and why what happened to them happened. Autobiographies most commonly have numerous crises of character. Still, they end with the writer defeating their demons, or overcoming hardships, turning failures into successes. We read biography to gain insight into the subject's values, motivators, drivers and character.

As it is in novels and biographies, so it is in life. Our impact on people is primarily determined by character interaction with our talents, abilities, and personalities. The depths of our relationships are significantly affected by our depth of character. People will rely on and forgive us if, amongst all of our other quirks, we are people they can rely on to act with conviction, integrity, and loyalty. Colleagues, friends, and community members look to us for consistency in behaviour regardless of context. People will trust us to the extent that we are consistent in our decision-making under challenging circumstances.

Your character goes with you wherever you go. Whether at work, sports club, community service organization, or home, your family, friends, or colleagues know how far they can trust you.

Character is globally transferable, where consistency in living out positive character traits is respected. For example, if you live and work in a foreign country and different culture, you can learn about the cultural norms and workplace ethics, but you are ultimately known for your character – for what defines you, whether people see inherent strength or weakness in you. People in your new environment will forgive cultural blunders or work mistakes if they know they can trust you to try and do better the next time.

Academic research, anecdotal evidence, and personal experience testify to the impact of strength of character, which is the manifestation or outworking of a number of your most vital positive character attributes, and that is a manifestation of your values, which are reflected in your integrity, reliability and ability to work and live with others. We all display many positive characteristics (character-is-tics), with a combination of our strongest being that which people see and say, "John is a person of character", "Salim has strength of character", "that is so typical (characteristic) of Adrienne".   Others include observations such as, "Matt is so reliable", "Jade is so humble", "Enrico is such a leader", and "Tiffany's leadership is seen in perseverance, teamwork and kindness".

These are signature character traits – your values in action – your character strengths.

This book is about strengths in general and character strengths in particular. We believe that developing already demonstrated or self-evident strengths is the path to the most significant growth and advancement in your personal and work life.

The Growth Lab Team

Chapter 1: Positive psychology, productivity, meaning and purpose

We must start with understanding positive psychology, strengths psychology, and even the 'happiness' movement.

Strengths

Strengths psychology, also known as positive psychology, emerged as a distinct field of study in the late 1990s and early 2000s. It grew out of the dissatisfaction of psychologists and researchers with psychology's traditional focus on pathology and negative aspects of human behaviour, such as mental illness and dysfunction.

Proponents of strengths psychology believed that the field should also focus on the positive aspects of human behaviour, such as resilience, creativity, and optimal functioning. They argued that psychologists could help individuals and communities lead more fulfilling lives by studying what makes people thrive and succeed.

One of the pioneers of strengths psychology was Martin Seligman, a psychologist who served as the president of the American Psychological Association in 1998. Seligman is known for his work on learned helplessness and optimism and is considered one of the founders of positive psychology.

Seligman started to research, test, trial, and evaluate what happens when we focus on strengths, not weaknesses. He wanted to know what happens when we focus on how to make somebody believe in themselves more and not focus on how to fix what is broken.

In the early 2000s, Seligman and other psychologists, such as Christopher Peterson, developed a character strengths and virtues taxonomy. In addition, they conducted extensive research to identify the key strengths contributing to human flourishing and developed assessment tools to help individuals identify their strengths.

Today, strengths psychology is a thriving field used in various settings, including education, business, and personal coaching. Its focus on positive aspects of human behaviour has increased emphasis on well-being and flourishing. As a result, it has helped individuals and communities worldwide achieve greater success and satisfaction.

Happiness

Happiness is one of the key concepts in positive psychology. It is often defined as a subjective experience of positive emotions, such as joy, contentment, and satisfaction. Positive psychology researchers study the factors contributing to happiness, such as positive relationships, meaningful work, and a sense of purpose or meaning in life.

One of the key findings of positive psychology research is that happiness is not just a result of external circumstances, such as wealth or success, but also depends on internal factors, such as mindset, gratitude, and character strengths. For example, people with a growth mindset, which is the belief that they can develop their abilities through effort and perseverance, tend to be happier than those with a fixed mindset, which is the belief that their abilities are fixed and unchangeable.

Seligman wrote "Authentic Happiness" to guide readers to achieve greater happiness and well-being.

In the book, he argues that happiness is not just a matter of external circumstances but also depends on internal factors such as mindset, character strengths, and positive relationships. He proposes that individuals can cultivate their happiness by focusing on these internal factors and developing a more positive outlook.

The book includes a variety of practical exercises and assessments that readers can use to identify their own character strengths and work on building them up. Seligman also discusses the importance of positive relationships, mindfulness, and gratitude in promoting happiness and well-being.

Overall, "Authentic Happiness" is a comprehensive and practical guide to positive psychology and the science of happiness. It provides readers with many tools and strategies for cultivating greater happiness and well-being.

"Flourishing" is another concept introduced by Martin Seligman to describe a state of optimal human functioning and well-being. He reflects on 'Authentic Happiness' and believes there is more to Happiness than he wrote there. According to Seligman, flourishing is characterized by positive emotions, engagement, positive relationships, meaning, and accomplishment.

Positive emotions refer to experiences such as joy, gratitude, and contentment. Engagement refers to being fully absorbed and engaged in enjoyable and challenging activities. Positive relationships refer to having meaningful connections with others. In contrast, meaning refers to having a sense of purpose and direction in life. Finally, Accomplishment refers to achieving goals and accomplishments that are meaningful and fulfilling.

Seligman's research has shown that individuals who experience 'flourishing' tend to have better mental and physical health, higher life satisfaction, and more tremendous success in their personal and professional lives. As a result, flourishing has become an essential concept in positive psychology. It has been used to guide interventions and programs to promote well-being and optimal functioning in individuals and communities.

Overall, positive psychology offers a valuable perspective on happiness and well-being. Its insights and interventions can help individuals and communities lead more fulfilling and satisfying lives.

Character Strengths

Martin Seligman and Chris Peterson looked at character strengths from a psychological and values-based perspective, and the VIA Institute founders have pursued this strengths approach to life. Instead of categorizing us by what is wrong, they categorize us by what is strong.

As identified by positive psychology research, character strengths refer to an individual's positive traits and qualities, such as courage, kindness, gratitude, and creativity (and many more). These strengths are inherent to individuals and can be developed and nurtured over time.

Character strengths are typically defined as positive traits that are morally valued and contribute to an individual's personal growth, flourishing and overall sense of fulfilment.

I am sure you have heard people say somebody brings out the best in them. I'm sure that you have found and interactions with people that they bring out the best in you, or others say that you bring out the best in them.

In many cases, this is because you believe in what they are doing, manifesting who they are, what they believe, and, therefore, their values in action. We refer to values in action as character, and the most obvious value is a character strength.

Character strengths are one of the critical components of positive psychology, as they are seen as fundamental to human flourishing. For example, the VIA (Values in Action) Classification of Character Strengths identifies 24 character strengths organized into six broad categories: Wisdom and knowledge, courage, Humanity, Justice, Temperance, and Transcendence. These strengths are seen as inherently positive qualities that are valued by individuals and communities around the world.

Such strengths are central to positive psychology interventions, practices, and techniques to promote well-being and positive outcomes. For example, interventions often focus on cultivating and strengthening individual character strengths, such as gratitude, kindness, and curiosity. By enhancing these positive qualities, individuals can experience greater well-being, resilience, and life satisfaction.

According to the VIA (Values in Action) classification system developed by Seligman and Peterson, 24-character strengths are grouped into six categories:

Wisdom and Knowledge: creativity, curiosity, open-mindedness, love of learning, perspective.

Courage: bravery, perseverance, honesty, zest

Humanity: love, kindness, social intelligence

Justice: teamwork, fairness, leadership

Temperance: forgiveness, humility, prudence, self-regulation

Transcendence: appreciation of beauty and excellence, gratitude, hope, humour, spirituality

You can discover your VIA Character Strengths here

https://www.growthlab.pro.viasurvey.org

The author/s and The Growth Lab do not earn any fee from this test.

Real stories

Graham is excited by and passionate about his work. He has a photographic memory and a talent for consolidating information and communicating it to an audience entertainingly and educationally. He is a creative person who is musical but also eloquent and theatrical. He is driven by a need to understand what lies in the future and is dedicated to pursuing truth in a world of speculation. He has found his vocation as a public speaker and author who travels the world, earning a good living and being a better and happier person.

Garth is a medical doctor who discovered his calling to work in media when he was a trainee working in a clinic in rural South Africa. He could see that so many of the illnesses presenting at the clinic could have been prevented by the simple practice of hygienic disciplines, such as washing hands or treating a wound before it could become infected. These are basic examples; however, the principle behind it is he realized the reach and impact of using entertaining and engaging television to reach the broadest possible audience who would not be learning about primary healthcare through the classroom or books because they could not go to school or hadn't learned to read. Garth, therefore, has made the very most of his intellect and medical training while developing a talent for identifying stories to tell and particularly how to find the funding for his projects which have borne fruit in healthcare worldwide

Chapter 2: Character Strengths

Let us remind ourselves of the six categories of character strengths, which the VIA Institute has called Virtues. Then, we will look at each category, breaking it down into character traits.

Virtues

Wisdom

Courage

Humanity

Justice

Temperance

Transcendence

Horsepower

I recently had to explain to my daughter the complexities of driving a manual gearbox or what they would call a stick shift car in the United States. This is the alternative to an automatic gearbox, where the car will respond to how much you put your foot down rather than you having to judge how much power you need to get up an incline or how to use the gears to pull away gently from a standing state, or to slow yourself down when on a steep descent.

As a lapsed ship's engineer, I couldn't help but explain it by referencing how we used to measure the power output of engines, as in horse power. I said that in different situations, you need to have a certain number of horses but that it is the responsibility of the driver of the cart to judge how much rein or encouragement the horses need in a given situation.

I can't help but use the same analogy of horses pulling a cart when explaining why some character attributes or strengths could or should be developed at a greater pace than what might be considered the character weaknesses or flaws.

When hitching horses to a cart, the usual practice is to put the strongest horses before the weaker ones. This arrangement helps to distribute the load evenly among the horses. It prevents any one horse from bearing too much of the burden. Additionally, putting stronger horses in front can help to set a steady pace for the team, which can be helpful when navigating rugged terrain or travelling long distances. However, the exact arrangement of the horses may vary depending on the specific circumstances and the preferences of the driver or handler.

Most helpful metaphors fail us at some point, but at its simplest, putting your signature strengths ahead of your secondary strengths at the front of your team of horses is quite helpful.

When you do any of these strength tests, you will come out with a certain number at the top of the list, which is clearly a stronger grouping than those that follow them. These are your signature strengths, which come easiest to you and which you feel most comfortable exercising in the workplace. You would use these strengths as often as possible in your work, community, and family responsibilities. Still, you won't rest on your laurels. You need to find ways to develop those strengths that are following them or which you feel you want to focus on, even if they are not at the top of your list.

If you transfer this back to the horses pulling the cart, you will see why playing to your signature strengths in the front row of your team of horses with those slightly less strong in the second row makes sense.

Without stretching the analogy too far, you might choose to have one of the weaker horses tethered to the back of the cart if it can keep up if it's not having to carry the load. Still, it can keep the pace while it gets stronger. On the other hand, suppose you stop the cart and focus only on getting the weak horse strong enough to pull. In that case, you will be frustrated as you don't get to use your signature strengths, and they will become unaccustomed to working for a living.

This is what we are doing when we do one of the strengths analysis tests and when we look at what we can use at the earliest convenience and opportunity and develop as we go along.

Wisdom

Creativity

Curiosity

Open-mindedness

Love of learning

Perspective

Wisdom and Knowledge

The character strengths in the Wisdom and Knowledge category are centred around the pursuit of knowledge, the ability to think critically, and the capacity to make sound judgments. In addition, these strengths are associated with intellectual curiosity, creativity, and an appreciation for new ideas and experiences. Here are the five character strengths in the Wisdom and Knowledge category:

Creativity is the ability to generate novel and useful ideas or solutions. It involves breaking free from conventional thinking methods to develop new perspectives and insights.

Curiosity is an active interest in learning new things and exploring the world. It involves a willingness to ask questions, seek answers, and remain open-minded to new possibilities.

Open-mindedness involves being receptive to new ideas and perspectives and being willing to consider alternative viewpoints. In addition, it requires a willingness to challenge one's assumptions and biases.

Love of learning is a strong desire to acquire new knowledge and skills and to continuously improve oneself through education and personal growth.

Perspective involves the ability to see things from multiple viewpoints and to consider diverse perspectives when making decisions. It allows individuals to approach problems and challenges more nuanced and thoughtfully.

Individuals with these character strengths tend to be curious, imaginative, innovative, and reflective. They can think critically, weigh evidence, and make sound judgments. They are also open to new experiences, love learning, and can see things from multiple perspectives.

Courage

Bravery

Perseverance

Honesty

Zest

Courage

The character strengths in the Courage category are centred around facing challenges, persevering in adversity, and acting with integrity and honesty. In addition, these strengths are associated with bravery, resilience, and the willingness to take risks. Here are the four character strengths in the Courage category:

Bravery faces fear, uncertainty, and danger with courage and determination. It involves taking risks, standing up for what is right, and persevering in adversity.

Perseverance persists in pursuing a goal, even in the face of obstacles or setbacks. It involves maintaining focus and motivation and staying committed to a task or objective over time.

Honesty involves being truthful, straightforward, and sincere in all interactions. It involves a willingness to admit mistakes, take responsibility for actions, and maintain integrity in all situations.

Zest is a sense of enthusiasm, energy, and excitement for life. It involves approaching new experiences positively and taking pleasure in the present moment.

Individuals with these character strengths are resilient, confident, and action-oriented. They can face challenges with courage, maintain their focus and motivation in the face of setbacks, and act with integrity and honesty. They can also approach new experiences with enthusiasm and excitement, often seen as inspiring and motivating to others. Individuals can enhance their resilience, overcome obstacles, and achieve tremendous success and fulfilment by cultivating these character strengths.

Humanity

Kindness

Love

Social Intelligence

Humanity

The strengths in the Humanity category are centred around connecting with and caring for others. They are associated with kindness, empathy, and the ability to build and maintain positive relationships.

Here are the three character strengths in the Humanity category:

Kindness involves being compassionate, empathetic, and helpful towards others. It involves a willingness to put the needs of others before oneself and to act in a caring and generous way.

Love manifests as deep and meaningful connections with others. It involves feeling a sense of warmth, affection, and appreciation towards others and being willing to express and act on these feelings.

Social intelligence is evident in the understanding and navigating of social situations effectively. It involves being able to perceive the emotions and perspectives of others and to respond appropriately to their needs and expectations.

Individuals with these character strengths tend to be caring, empathetic, and supportive towards others. As a result, they can form strong and positive relationships and connect with others meaningfully. They are also skilled at understanding and navigating social situations and are often seen as helpful and supportive members of their communities.

By cultivating these character strengths, individuals can enhance their interpersonal skills, improve their relationships, and contribute to the well-being of others.

Justice

Fairness

Teamwork

Leadership

Citizenship

Justice

The justice category centres around promoting fairness, equality, and ethical behaviour. These strengths are associated with a sense of responsibility towards others, a desire for social harmony, and a commitment to upholding moral principles.

Here are the four character strengths in the Justice category:

Fairness involves treating others equitably and justly and being willing to act impartially and unbiasedly. It involves a commitment to upholding principles of justice and equality and promoting the welfare of all individuals.

Leadership inspires and guides others towards a common goal or purpose. It involves making decisions, taking responsibility for one's actions, and acting honestly.

Teamwork involves working collaboratively with others towards a shared goal or objective. It involves communicating effectively, resolving conflicts, and contributing to the team's success.

Citizenship means being an active and responsible member of one's community and contributing to the welfare of society. It involves a commitment to upholding ethical and moral principles and taking action to promote social justice and equality.

Individuals with these strengths are responsible, ethical, and committed to promoting fairness and justice. They lead and motivate others towards a common goal and work collaboratively towards a shared objective. They are also active and responsible members of their communities and work to promote social justice and equality. Nurturing these character strengths, individuals can become more effective leaders, improve their communication and teamwork skills, and contribute to the well-being of society.

Temperance

Forgiveness

Humility

Prudence

Self-Regulation

Temperance

The character strengths in the Temperance category are centred around the ability to regulate one's emotions, desires, and actions. In addition, these strengths are associated with self-control, moderation, and the ability to resist temptations and impulses.

Here are the four character strengths in the Temperance category:

Forgiveness lets go of anger, resentment, and bitterness towards others and moves on from past hurts. It involves a willingness to understand and empathize with others and to forgive them for their mistakes and shortcomings.

Humility is a modest and respectful attitude towards oneself and others. It involves recognizing one's own limitations and imperfections and being able to learn from the feedback and criticism of others.

Prudence is evident in wise and cautious decisions and in avoiding impulsive or risky behaviour. It involves considering the potential consequences of one's actions and taking steps to minimize risks and maximize benefits.

Self-regulation includes controlling one's thoughts, emotions, and behaviours to achieve long-term goals. It involves resisting temptations and impulses and delaying gratification in pursuing more meaningful and fulfilling outcomes.

Individuals with these character strengths are self-disciplined, self-aware, and effectively regulate their thoughts, emotions, and behaviours. They forgive others, let go of past hurts, and are modest and respectful in their interactions. They make wise, cautious decisions and resist temptations and impulses to achieve long-term goals.

Transcendence

Appreciation of Beauty and Excellence

Gratitude

Hope

Humour

Spirituality

Transcendence

The character strengths in the Transcendence category are centred around connecting with something larger than oneself. In addition, these strengths are associated with a sense of purpose, meaning, and spirituality.

Here are the five character strengths in the Transcendence category:

Appreciation of beauty and excellence recognizes and appreciates the beauty, excellence, and skill in the world around us. It evokes a sense of awe, wonder, and appreciation for the finer things in life.

Gratitude manifests in being thankful for the positive aspects of one's life and expressing this gratitude to others. It involves a sense of appreciation for the good things in life and a willingness to acknowledge and express this appreciation.

Hope maintains a positive outlook towards the future, believing that positive change is possible. It brings a sense of optimism and a belief in one's ability to overcome obstacles and achieve one's goals.

Humour finds amusement in everyday situations, even in adversity or difficulty. It does not deny hardship but contributes a sense of playfulness and the ability to see the lighter side of life.

Spirituality is a connection to something larger than oneself, whether a higher power, nature, or community. It involves a sense of purpose and meaning and a belief in the interconnectedness of all things.

Individuals with these character strengths tend to be connected to a larger purpose and meaning. They can appreciate the beauty and excellence in the world around them. They are also grateful for the positive aspects of their lives and maintain a positive outlook towards the future. They can find humour and amusement in everyday situations. They may have a spiritual or religious belief system providing a sense of purpose and meaning.

Individuals can enhance their sense of purpose, meaning, and well-being by cultivating these character strengths and connecting with something larger than themselves.

Chapter 3: Character Flaws

At this juncture of the book, you might wonder why we're emphasizing the development of character strengths without discussing character weaknesses or flaws. To shed light on this, let's pause and contemplate what character weaknesses or flaws often signify. Our fundamental premise is that character strength or positive character traits, reflect our values. Consequently, when we witness counterproductive, hurtful, and even harmful behaviours, such as anti-social behaviour, we witness a manifestation of values or beliefs that have arisen through a troubled past.

The Arbinger Institute write in the Anatomy of Peace about four fundamental beliefs, which underly a conflict mindset, or the 'Heart at War' mindset, and can manifest as character weakness – or a public display of flawed values in action.

Heart at War

I am better than you

I am worse than you

I deserve what you have

I do not deserve what you have

I am better than you.

When we compare ourselves to others and see ourselves as superior, we may feel a sense of self-satisfaction or pride, but this can also lead to a lack of empathy, respect, and collaboration with others.

The "Heart at War" mentality is characterized by focusing on one's needs and desires at the expense of others and viewing others as obstacles or threats to one's goals and interests. When we adopt a mindset of superiority, we may see others as less important or less valuable than ourselves, which can lead to conflict and adverse outcomes.

The premise of positive psychology is that instead of focusing on fixing the weakness or addressing the pain, you might seek to include the wounded individual in positive activities which show them in an actual situation that they can make a difference in the lives of others through looking beyond themselves, even if only for a moment. While emphasising the fruits of positive behaviour, any intervention dealing with the underlying pain is within a growth environment and not a deficit perspective.

For example, adopting a "Heart at Peace" mindset is helpful, emphasising empathy, respect, and a willingness to listen and collaborate with others. This means recognizing the unique strengths and contributions of others and working together towards common goals.

By adopting a mindset of collaboration and cooperation, we can build stronger relationships, achieve greater success, and create a more positive and productive environment for everyone involved.

I am worse than you.

The 'worse than you' perspective reflects a sense of inferiority and a focus on comparisons and competition with others. This mindset can lead to feelings of resentment, envy, and self-doubt. It may prevent individuals from recognizing their own strengths and unique contributions.

A strengths intervention avoids focusing on comparisons and competition. Instead, it is more helpful to focus on personal growth and development and to strive to be the best version of oneself.

I deserve what you have.

When you have unfulfilled wants that you see others have satisfied, it implies a sense of entitlement and a focus on one's own needs and desires at the expense of others. This mindset can lead to conflict and negative outcomes, as it may prevent individuals from considering the perspectives and needs of others.

A "Heart at Peace" intervention emphasizes empathy, respect, and a willingness to listen and collaborate with others. This means recognizing that everyone has unique needs and desires and deserves to be treated with dignity and respect. Rather than focusing solely on one's desires, it is essential to consider the perspectives and needs of others and to work together towards mutually beneficial solutions.

I do not deserve what you have.

Feeling undeserving reflects a sense of unworthiness and a lack of self-esteem. We may feel inadequate or powerless when we believe we do not deserve good things, leading to negative outcomes.

When the behaviour, flawed values in action, is based on unworthiness, intervention emphasizes self-worth and self-care while recognizing the value and worth of others. This means valuing oneself and one's contributions while also recognizing and respecting the unique strengths and contributions of others. By recognizing one's worth and treating oneself with kindness and compassion, individuals can build stronger self-esteem and resilience, leading to greater success and fulfilment in all areas of life.

You can see how the preceding distorted views of self and others will present as a flawed character in antisocial, argumentative, and controlling behaviours. They are displayed by cynicism and sarcasm, and disrespect. You see evidence of a flawed worldview when you find people who are jealous, arrogant, and manipulative. Flawed character shows inappropriate obsession, pessimism, and prejudice. People can show themselves to be selfish, self-centred, temperamental, and uncooperative.

When we encounter the above behaviours in the workplace, we can spend a lot of time and energy trying to address those weaknesses, or we could seek to include those individuals in positive and affirming, and engaging activities if we can only determine a couple of those parts of their lives which are unique strengths. As we say throughout the book, nothing is better than finding meaning in our work. We are enabled through training, coaching, mentoring, and encouragement to do what we can and contribute to the team.

This is not a blanket abdication of your responsibility as a manager. You must also explain what behaviours are counterproductive to your work environment and put a plan in place to measure performance and impact on the work environment overtime. You will invest in helping those people find counselling when appropriate. Still, we all recognise that managers have a duty to their employer to manage their employees to further the business's good and discipline those who do not.

Overall, character strengths are an essential element of positive psychology. They represent a positive and strengths-based approach to understanding human experience and promoting well-being. Positive psychology promotes optimal functioning and flourishing at individual and community levels by focusing on what is best in people and encouraging the development and expression of their inherent strengths and virtues.

Strength of character and character strengths

"Strength of character" and "character strengths" are related but distinct concepts.

Strength of character refers to the overall quality of an individual's moral and ethical principles, including integrity, honesty, and loyalty. It measures an individual's moral fortitude and the extent to which they adhere to ethical principles and values.

While strength of character and character strengths are essential aspects of an individual's character, they are distinct concepts. Strength of character is a broader concept encompassing an individual's moral principles and values. In contrast, character strengths are specific traits and abilities contributing to an individual's positive psychological functioning. Both are important for personal growth and success in life. Still, they refer to different aspects of an individual's character, personality, and motivators.

A person with a strong character consistently acts by their principles and values, even in the face of adversity or temptation. They have a sense of purpose and direction in life. They are committed to living a life guided by their moral and ethical beliefs.

Strength of character is often considered an essential component of personal and professional success. Individuals with strong character are more likely to be respected and trusted by others. They are often seen as role models or leaders within their communities. In addition, they are more likely to make ethical decisions and take responsibility for their actions, even under challenging circumstances.

Chapter 4: Clifton's Strengths

One of the leading proponents of a strengths-based approach to employee development and organizational growth is Marcus Buckingham, who co-wrote a book called, 'Now, Discover Your Strengths', with Donald O. Clifton.

Clifton, a psychologist and entrepreneur, developed the CliftonStrengths assessment, previously known as the StrengthsFinder, identifying individuals' unique strengths and talents.

The book's initial chapter, titled "The Revolution," begins by asserting that the best organizations do not merely acknowledge the individual differences of their employees but actively leverage these differences. Instead, the focus should be on identifying each employee's natural talents and then positioning and cultivating them to transform these abilities into genuine strengths.

While employed at the Gallup organization, a survey of 198,000 employees across 7,939 business units and 36 companies was conducted. The primary inquiry was whether employees had the chance to utilize their strengths daily. The outcomes were then compared to the performance of each business unit.

The results revealed that employees who strongly concurred with having the opportunity to use their strengths daily were twice as likely to work in business units with lower employee turnover. Additionally, these business units demonstrated increased productivity and customer satisfaction scores.

After surveying over 1.7 million employees worldwide, Clifton and Buckingham discovered that only 20% of employees felt that their strengths were being utilized daily. Their research shows that the best managers believe in each person's talents' enduring and unique nature and that an individual's greatest growth potential lies within their strongest areas. These insights are elaborated in the book 'First, Break all the Rules', which precedes the one in question.

It is crucial to capitalize on our strengths. Therefore, identifying and investing in further developing our strengths is necessary while not ignoring our weaknesses altogether. Conventional wisdom suggests we should focus on our weaknesses and rely on our strengths to carry us through. However, research, such as that conducted by Buckingham, demonstrates that developing and utilizing our strengths is crucial to our growth and success, even while addressing our weaknesses.

Buckingham and Clifton have created an online tool called the StrengthsFinder, which identifies an individual's five signature strengths from a pool of thirty-four they have identified. They more accurately refer to them as signature themes.

The authors introduce three critical terms crucial to understanding the concept of strengths.

The first term is "talents," which refers to recurring patterns of thought and feeling. First, however, they clarify that the themes of talent measured by the StrengthsFinder profile determine an individual's five signature strengths.

The second term is "knowledge," which encompasses facts and lessons learned.

Finally, they introduce "skills," which involve the steps necessary to complete an activity.

Combining these three factors - talents, knowledge, and skills - defines an individual's strengths.

The authors debunk the notion that success is solely a matter of mind over matter or that one can achieve anything simply by putting their mind to it. Instead, they emphasize the importance of identifying one's dominant talents or themes and then using knowledge and skills to refine and develop them.

According to Buckingham, a talent is any recurring pattern of thought, feeling, or behaviour that can be applied productively. Examples of these talents include being instinctively curious, competitive, charming, or persistent. Any pattern of thought, feeling, or behaviour that can be identified and utilized constitutes a talent.

Overall, the CliftonStrengths assessment aims to help individuals recognize and harness their strengths rather than focus solely on improving weaknesses. As a result, individuals can improve their performance, relationships, and overall well-being by understanding and utilizing their strengths.

The assessment can be done here:

https://www.gallup.com/cliftonstrengths/en/254033/strengths finder.aspx

The author/s and The Growth Lab do not earn any fee from this test.

The 34 Clifton Strengths:

- Achiever
- Activator
- Adaptability
- Analytical
- Arranger
- Belief
- Command
- Communication
- Competition
- Connectedness
- Consistency
- Context
- Deliberative
- Developer
- Empathy
- Focus
- Futuristic
- Harmony
- Ideation
- Includer
- Individualization
- Input
- Intellection
- Learner
- Maximizer
- Positivity
- Relator
- Responsibility
- Restorative
- Self-Assurance
- Significance
- Strategic
- Woo

These strengths are divided into four categories: executing, influencing, relationship building, and strategic thinking. Each category comprises 8 or 9 themes representing individuals' strengths and talents.

Strengths Categorization

Executing

Influencing

Relationship Building

Strategic Thinking

Executing

Achiever

Arranger

Belief

Consistency

Deliberative

Discipline

Focus

Responsibility

Restorative

Executing:

These are the strengths that involve making things happen. For example, people with strengths in this domain are often action-oriented, practical, and reliable.

Achiever: Their drive to achieve goals and high stamina.

Arranger: Your ability to organize and create structure, often finding innovative ways to make things work.

Belief: They are guided by strong personal values, beliefs, and principles and have a strong sense of purpose.

Consistency: Your commitment to fairness, treating everyone equally, and having an eye for details that others may overlook.

Deliberative: Methodical and careful, weighing all options before taking action.

Discipline: They have a strong sense of structure and routine and can establish clear rules and boundaries for themselves and others.

Focus: Our ability to prioritize and concentrate on a specific task, goal, or vision for an extended period without distraction.

Responsibility: Your sense of accountability for your actions and the willingness to take ownership of assigned responsibilities.

Restorative: Your ability and inclination to solve problems, especially when overcoming obstacles or fixing broken things.

Influencing

Activator

Command

Communication

Competition

Maximizer

Self-Assurance

Significance

Woo

Influencing:

These are the strengths that involve influencing others. People with strengths in this domain are often enthusiastic, persuasive, and engaging.

Activator: Energetic and enthusiastic, taking the initiative and getting things done.

Command: Your ability to take charge and lead, making decisions with confidence.

Communication: Skilled at conveying ideas and thoughts to others, making complex topics understandable.

Competition: Highly driven by challenges and comparison to others, striving to be the best.

Maximizer: Focused on strengths and finding ways to enhance them, often turning good into great.

Self-Assurance: Your strong belief in your abilities, ideas, and judgments.

Significance: Our desire to be recognized as important, influential, and significant by others.

Woo: "Winning Others Over." People with this strength naturally connect with others and persuade them to join their causes or ideas.

Relationship Building

Adaptability

Connectedness

Developer

Empathy

Harmony

Includer

Individualization

Positivity

Relator

Relationship Building:

These are the strengths that involve building and maintaining relationships. People with strengths in this domain are often empathetic, supportive, and authentic.

Adaptability: Flexible and adaptable, able to quickly adjust to changing circumstances.

Connectedness: Their strong sense of interconnectedness and believe that everything is somehow connected.

Developer: Our ability to recognize and develop potential in others, often serving as a mentor or coach.

Empathy: Being highly in tune with others' emotions and able to see things from their perspective.

Harmony: Their skill in creating peaceful and harmonious environments and relationships.

Includer: Your ability and tendency to include others in a group or situation, regardless of their background or status.

Individualization: Our ability to recognize and appreciate each individual's unique qualities and characteristics.

Positivity: They tend to be optimistic and see life's bright side. People with this strength are generally enthusiastic, upbeat, and energetic.

Relator: Our ability and preference for developing close, meaningful, and enduring relationships with others.

Strategic Thinking

Analytical

Context

Futuristic

Ideation

Input

Intellection

Learner

Strategic

Strategic Thinking:

These are the strengths that involve analyzing information and developing strategies. People with strengths in this domain are often logical, innovative, and future-oriented.

Analytical: Skilled at breaking down complex information and making connections between seemingly disparate pieces of information.

Context: Understanding the present by researching and learning from the past.

Futuristic: Your keen sense of imagination and vision for the future.

Ideation: Highly creative, generating and conceptualizing new ideas quickly.

Input: They strongly desire to collect and gather information, often becoming experts in their chosen field.

Intellection: Your natural tendency to engage in deep and reflective thinking.

Learner: Our strong desire and ability to continuously acquire new knowledge and skills.

Strategic: Their ability to think and plan strategically. Individuals with this strength are good at seeing the big picture, identifying patterns and connections, and thinking outside the box to develop innovative solutions.

When we use our strengths, we feel more engaged with our work, colleagues, company, family, friends, and community. Therefore, it's crucial to identify our strengths and seek opportunities that allow us to utilize them at least 60 or 70% of the time.

While it's unrealistic to expect a job that utilizes all of our strengths all the time, we must aim to use most of our strengths, most of the time, for the benefit of everyone involved.

Chapter 5: Mapping VIA Character Strengths

PERMA

MBTI

Clifton

PERMA

Positive Emotion

Engagement

Relationships

Meaning

Accomplishment

Mapping to Flourishing PERMA

Character strengths and Seligman's PERMA are frameworks for understanding human well-being and flourishing. Still, they differ in their focus and scope.

While character strengths and PERMA focus on positive aspects of human experience, they differ in specificity. Character strengths are more narrowly focused on individual traits and qualities. At the same time, PERMA is more broad and holistic, encompassing multiple domains of human experience.

On the other hand, Seligman's PERMA is a framework for understanding well-being that includes five core elements: Positive emotion, Engagement, Relationships, Meaning, and Accomplishment. These elements are seen as critical components of a fulfilling and meaningful life. Moreover, they are universal across cultures and contexts.

Another difference is that character strengths are seen as inherent to individuals. At the same time, PERMA is viewed as a set of conditions that can be cultivated and nurtured over time. In this sense, PERMA focuses more on the external factors contributing to well-being. At the same time, character strengths are seen as internal qualities contributing to personal growth and flourishing.

Overall, while there is some overlap between character strengths and PERMA, they are distinct frameworks that offer different perspectives on human well-being and flourishing.

Mapping Character strengths to MBTI

While there is no direct mapping between character strengths and Myers-Briggs types, exploring how character strengths may align with personality traits and preferences is possible.

For example, individuals who score high on the Myers-Briggs Type Indicator (MBTI) dimension of extraversion may be more likely to exhibit character strengths such as enthusiasm, social intelligence, and humour. Conversely, individuals who score high on the MBTI dimension of introversion may be more likely to exhibit character strengths such as gratitude, curiosity, and perspective.

Similarly, individuals who score high on the MBTI dimension of sensing may be more likely to exhibit character strengths such as practicality, humility, and attention to detail. On the other hand, those who score high on the intuition dimension may be more likely to exhibit character strengths such as creativity, curiosity, and perspective.

Individuals who score high on the MBTI dimension of thinking may be more likely to exhibit character strengths such as critical thinking, honesty, and leadership. Conversely, those scoring high on the feeling dimension may be likelier to exhibit character strengths such as kindness, empathy, and teamwork.

While there is no direct mapping between character strengths and Myers-Briggs types, exploring how character strengths may align with personality traits and preferences is possible. By understanding how different strengths and traits are related, individuals can gain insights into their strengths and areas for development, as well as strategies for maximizing their potential and achieving their goals.

Mapping Clifton's and the Character Strengths

They are both frameworks that focus on identifying and leveraging strengths instead of focusing on the development of weaknesses.

Here are some critical differences between the two:

Methodology: Clifton's Strengths are identified through the StrengthsFinder assessment, which is based on a set of 34 talent themes, while Character Strengths are identified through the VIA Classification of Character Strengths, which is based on 24 universal strengths that are recognized and valued across cultures.

Valuation: Although all strengths apply to all areas of our life, meaning, and purpose, it might be fair to say Clifton's Strengths are more oriented towards performance and productivity, while Character Strengths are more oriented towards personal impact and well-being.

Integration: Again, at the risk of creating an artificial distinction, Clifton's Strengths can be integrated into an individual's work and career, while Character Strengths can be integrated into an individual's overall sense of purpose and meaning.

In summary, while both frameworks share similarities in their focus on identifying and leveraging strengths, their methodology, context, and valuation differ. Clifton's Strengths primarily focus on individual strengths in the workplace (or 'output-driven') context. In contrast, Character Strengths focus on expressions of our values everywhere. These strengths can be applied to various contexts for personal growth, well-being and performance at work.

The VIA Character Coefficient

Our character is the essence of who we are and what others see. Our character is our values in action, hence the VIA acronym of the VIA Institute on character. The abbreviation VIA has now evolved to mean getting from one point to the other through another location. So you go VIA one city to get to another.

In the same way, we have talents and aptitudes that make us strong performers in our chosen pursuits. You might know what our abilities are. Possibly our job doesn't provide opportunity nor evidence to display our practical and intellectual, and emotional strengths. Some positions require us to suppress our natural talents because they would negatively impact the job. Our creativity will not improve the situation in our daily tasks if we are a worker on an assembly line. Still, it might help us to consider improving efficiency and saving the company money. Creativity may be central to our job in advertising. Still, if we can bring our other strength of prudence into play, we might produce copy that appeals to a broader audience.

Our character combines with our talents to produce results. Just as we are a unique combination of skills, our character combines positive and negative character traits. Our performance results from how they are combined with our personality types.

When our character strengths and talent themes / strengths complement each other, we have the 'character coefficient' – the multiplier of character over and above our other talents and strengths.

Mapping Talent Themes

Matching character strengths with Clifton's strengths indicator, here are some possible matches between the character strengths and Clifton's talent themes:

Creativity: "Ideation" - This talent theme refers to an individual's ability to generate new and innovative ideas.

Curiosity: "Learner" - This theme refers to a person's love of learning and desire to continuously improve their knowledge and skills.

Love of learning: "Input" – 'Input' refers to an individual's natural curiosity and desire to gather and absorb information.

Bravery: "Courage" refers to an individual's ability to face challenges and take risks, even in fear or uncertainty.

Honesty: "Integrity" – 'Integrity' refers to an individual's commitment to honesty, fairness, and ethical behaviour.

Kindness: "Empathy" - This talent theme refers to an individual's ability to sense and understand the feelings and perspectives of others and to respond with compassion and kindness.

It's worth noting that there is not always a one-to-one correspondence between character strengths and Clifton's talent themes, as these frameworks are based on different conceptualizations of human strengths and abilities. However, there is some overlap between the two. Both can be valuable tools for understanding and developing one's strengths and abilities.

In the above section, we took the perspective of finding talent themes that mapped with the character strength we listed.

In the next section, we take the opposite perspective of looking for character strengths that match the talent theme listed.

Mapping Character Strengths

Clifton's Strengths and Character Strengths are different frameworks focusing on personal strengths. However, some talent themes from the StrengthsFinder assessment are similar to character strengths from the VIA Classification of Character Strengths. Here are some examples:

Achiever - "Perseverance," which involves the ability to persist in facing challenges and obstacles, is similar to the Achiever theme. People with the Achiever talent theme have a strong work ethic and are driven to accomplish tasks and goals. They are willing to put in the necessary effort to achieve success. They are not easily deterred by setbacks or failures.

Learner - The character strength of "Love of Learning," which is the desire to continuously acquire new knowledge and skills, is like Clifton's Learner. People with the Learner talent theme have a thirst for knowledge and are constantly seeking opportunities to learn and grow. They enjoy exploring new topics and ideas and are often self-directed.

Strategic - "Wisdom," involving critical thinking and making sound decisions, aligns with the Strategic talent theme. People with the Strategic talent theme can think strategically and consider multiple options. In addition, they are good at anticipating potential challenges and developing contingency plans.

Empathy is similar to the character strength of "Kindness," showing care and concern for others. People with the Empathy talent theme can understand and relate to the feelings and perspectives of others. They are skilled at building relationships and are often seen as caring and compassionate.

Harmony - Similar to the character strength of "Fairness," which involves treating people equitably and impartially. People with the Harmony talent theme can create a sense of harmony and consensus among groups. They are good at understanding different perspectives and finding common ground.

Maximizer - The character strength of "Excellence," which involves pursuing high standards and continuous improvement, clearly complements the Maximizer. People with the Maximizer talent theme can identify and capitalize on their and others' strengths. They desire to continuously improve and are often focused on achieving excellence.

While these six talent themes have similarities with character strengths, it's important to note the differences between the two frameworks. The VIA Classification of Character Strengths is based on 24 universal strengths valued across cultures and contexts. At the same time, the StrengthsFinder assessment focuses on individual talents that can be leveraged for success in the workplace. Additionally, the VIA Classification is often used for personal growth and development. In contrast, the StrengthsFinder assessment is primarily used in the workplace.

Chapter 6: Personal Development

Personal development and character strengths are closely related, as personal development often involves identifying and leveraging one's character strengths to achieve personal and professional goals. Here's an overview of personal development and character strengths:

Identifying strengths: The first step in leveraging character strengths for personal development is identifying one's strengths. This can be done through self-reflection or assessments such as the VIA Survey of Character Strengths.

Setting goals: Personal growth often involves setting goals and working towards them. When setting goals, it's important to consider character strengths and how they can be leveraged to achieve them.

Overcoming challenges: Career advancement involves demonstrably overcoming challenges and obstacles. Individuals can more effectively overcome challenges and achieve their goals by leveraging character strengths such as perseverance, creativity, and courage.

Building resilience: Personal development can also involve building resilience, which is the ability to bounce back from challenges and setbacks. Individuals can build resilience and better cope with stress and adversity by leveraging character strengths such as optimism, gratitude, and social support.

Self-awareness: Advancement involves self-awareness, which is the ability to understand one's own thoughts, feelings, and behaviours. By leveraging character strengths such as self-awareness, individuals can more effectively identify areas for personal growth and development.

Using character strengths for personal development and career advancement can bring a wide range of benefits, including:

Increased self-awareness: By identifying and reflecting on your character strengths, you can gain a deeper understanding of your own values, motivations, and natural abilities.

Improved self-esteem and confidence: Focusing on your strengths can help you feel more confident and capable, positively impacting your self-esteem.

Increased resilience: Building on your strengths can help you become more resilient in facing challenges and setbacks.

Enhanced well-being: Research has shown that character strengths are associated with increased well-being and life satisfaction.

Improved relationships: By understanding your strengths and those of others, you can build stronger, more positive relationships with those in your life.

Greater career satisfaction: Using your strengths in your career can lead to increased job satisfaction and career success.

Personal growth and development: Focusing on your strengths can help you identify areas for growth and development, which can lead to personal and professional growth over time.

Overall, personal development and character strengths are closely related. Therefore, identifying and leveraging one's character strengths can be crucial in achieving personal and professional goals, building resilience, and overcoming challenges.

Flow

This is an excellent place to discuss the concept of 'Flow' as another compelling reason to find your strengths and use them daily. When you are using your strengths on tasks that interest you, there is a good chance you enter states of flow from time to time. On the other hand, using your strengths on uninteresting tasks may be necessary for the team or organization, but you are not likely to enter a state of flow.

Imagine hours or even days in the Flow state. You pursue this when looking for meaningful work that matches your strengths.

Flow is a state of optimal experience where a person is fully immersed and absorbed in an activity, feeling energized and focused, and losing track of time. This concept was introduced by psychologist Mihaly Csikszentmihalyi in his book "Flow: The Psychology of Optimal Experience," published in 1990. Csikszentmihalyi argues that this flow state is essential for happiness and fulfilment in life. He provides numerous examples from different fields, such as sports, music, art, and work, to illustrate how people can achieve flow.

Csikszentmihalyi identifies several factors that contribute to the experience of flow, such as having clear goals, receiving immediate feedback, facing challenges that match one's skills, and being fully present in the moment. He also explores how flow can be applied in different domains, such as education, business, and social relationships, to enhance performance, creativity, and well-being.

The concept of flow can be applied to being happy at work because it involves experiencing a state of optimal engagement and enjoyment in one's work. When people experience flow at work, they feel fulfilled and satisfied. They are more likely to be productive, creative, and committed to their jobs.

Here are some ways that flow can contribute to happiness at work:

Clear goals and feedback: To experience flow, individuals must have clear goals and receive immediate feedback on their progress. In a work setting, employees should clearly understand what they need to accomplish, how their work contributes to the organization's overall goals, and how their performance is evaluated. In addition, employees who receive regular feedback and recognition for their efforts are more likely to feel a sense of accomplishment and satisfaction.

Challenging tasks: Flow occurs when you are engaged in challenging tasks but still within your skill level. In a work setting, employees should be given tasks that are challenging enough to keep them engaged and motivated but not so complex that they feel overwhelmed or frustrated. When employees are given tasks that match their skills and abilities, they are more likely to experience a sense of mastery and fulfilment.

Autonomy and control: Flow is more likely to occur when you have a sense of autonomy and control over your work. In a work setting, employees should be given some control over their work schedule, tasks, and how they approach their work. Employees with a sense of autonomy and control are likelier to feel motivated and invested in their work.

Collaboration and support: Flow can also be facilitated by collaboration and support from others. In a work setting, employees should be encouraged to work in teams, communicate effectively, and receive support from their colleagues and supervisors. When employees feel supported and connected to others, they are more likely to experience a sense of community and belonging.

Your character strengths

Identifying and developing individual character strengths involves a few steps:

Self-reflection: The first step is self-reflection to identify your character strengths. You can ask yourself questions such as: What do I enjoy doing? What activities do I excel at? What comes naturally to me? What do I feel passionate about?

Take an assessment: Another way to identify your character strengths is to take an assessment. One is the VIA Survey of Character Strengths, a free online assessment that identifies your top character strengths.

Get feedback from others: You can also ask for feedback from people who know you well, such as friends, family members, or colleagues. They may be able to identify strengths that you may not have considered.

Develop your strengths: Once you have identified your character strengths, the next step is to develop and strengthen them. This can be done through intentional practice and seeking opportunities to use your strengths in various areas of life. For example, suppose you have identified a strength of creativity. In that case, you may want to explore creative hobbies or seek creative projects at work.

Use your strengths in new ways: It's also essential to use them in new and different ways to continue developing and strengthening them. For example, suppose you have identified a leadership strength. In that case, you may seek opportunities to lead new projects or initiatives at work.

Seek feedback: Finally, seeking feedback from others is vital to help you continue developing and refining your strengths. This can be done by asking for colleague feedback or seeking a mentor who can provide guidance and support.

By following these steps, you can identify and develop your individual character strengths, which can help you achieve personal and professional goals, build resilience, and overcome challenges.

A strengths-based career path

Building a strengths-based career path involves identifying and using your unique character strengths to guide your career choices and development. Here are some steps you can take:

Identify your strengths: Start by identifying your character strengths using tools such as the VIA Survey of Character Strengths or by reflecting on your own experiences and feedback from others.

Consider your career goals: Next, consider your goals and how your strengths can help you achieve them. Think about the kinds of work you enjoy and are naturally good at and what motivates you.

Find roles that align with your strengths: Look for job roles that align with your strengths and consider how you can use them in those roles. You can do this by researching job descriptions and company culture to identify roles and organizations that value and support the use of character strengths.

Develop your strengths: Once you have identified them, focus on developing and refining them. This can be done through training, seeking out challenging assignments, and seeking feedback and mentorship from others.

Build a portfolio: As you develop your strengths, consider building a portfolio of accomplishments and evidence showcasing your strengths. This can help you demonstrate your value to potential employers and advance your career.

Seek out opportunities to use your strengths: Finally, seek out opportunities to use your strengths in your current role or other areas of your life. This can help you build confidence and experience, expand your network and build new relationships.

By following these steps, you can build a strengths-based career path that is fulfilling, rewarding, and aligned with your unique strengths and values.

Using character strengths for personal development can lead to a more fulfilling, meaningful life and greater happiness and success.

Your signature strengths in the workplace

Applying character strengths in the workplace involves using your unique character strengths to enhance your performance, build stronger relationships with colleagues, and contribute to the success of your organization. Here are some ways you can apply character strengths in the workplace:

Identify your signature strengths: Start by using tools such as the VIA Survey of Character Strengths or by reflecting on your own experiences and feedback from others.

Apply your strengths to your work: Consider how to apply them once you have identified them. This might involve finding ways to use your strengths to enhance your performance in your current role or seeking opportunities to use your strengths in new projects or initiatives.

Communicate your strengths: Let your colleagues and managers know about your strengths and how to use them to benefit the team and organization. This can help you build stronger relationships with colleagues and position yourself as a valuable contributor to the team.

Support others in using their strengths: Look for ways to support your colleagues in using their own strengths. This might involve recognizing and celebrating their strengths or finding ways to help them apply them to their work.

Foster a strengths-based culture: Finally, work to foster a strengths-based culture in your organization. This can involve promoting character strengths in hiring, performance evaluations, and team-building activities and encouraging colleagues to identify and develop their strengths.

By applying character strengths in the workplace, you can enhance your performance, build stronger relationships with colleagues, and contribute to the success of your organization.

Chapter 7: Strengths in the workplace

The importance of character strengths falls under the same umbrella as the importance of opportunities to use our intellectual, emotional, personality, and practical strengths at work. A strengths perspective is advantageous in the workplace for several reasons:

By recognizing their strengths, employees can feel more confident and empowered to contribute to their organization meaningfully if given the opportunity to use them. In addition, knowing their inherent talents and character strengths helps individuals leverage these unique abilities and talents and seek careers or jobs that align with their values.

Research suggests that the identification and use of character strengths in the workplace can have numerous benefits, including:

Increased job satisfaction: Employees encouraged to use their character strengths in their work feel more engaged and satisfied.

Here, development focuses on developing employees' strengths rather than correcting weaknesses. Managers provide regular feedback and coaching to help employees maximize their strengths and develop new skills that complement their strengths.

When employees can use their strengths in their work and are recognized for their contributions, they are more likely to be satisfied with their jobs.

Improved employee engagement: A strengths-based culture can increase employee engagement by providing employees with a sense of purpose and fulfilment, allowing them to use their strengths and talents in their work.

Your employer culture values employees' unique strengths and talents and fosters collaboration and teamwork. It promotes employee well-being, diversity, and inclusion. A strengths-based culture values diversity and inclusion, recognizing that everyone brings unique strengths and perspectives to the workplace. This creates a more inclusive and supportive work environment where all employees feel valued and respected.

Employees are likelier to stay with an organization that values and recognizes their strengths, leading to improved retention rates.

Better teamwork: When employees understand and appreciate each other's strengths, they can work together, collaborate, and achieve shared goals. Employees are encouraged to collaborate and build on each other's strengths. Teams are formed based on complementary strengths rather than job titles or hierarchy.

Positive work environment: When workplaces prioritize developing and using character strengths, it can create a positive and supportive environment where individuals feel valued and respected. Employees who can use their strengths will likely perform better and more effectively.

Positive feedback: Managers and colleagues provide positive feedback to recognize and encourage using strengths. Celebrating successes and achievements is an integral part of the culture. In addition, they support professional development and growth. By focusing on strengths, employees can identify areas for improvement and work to develop new skills and abilities that complement their existing strengths.

Employee well-being: Employee well-being is prioritised and recognizes the importance of work-life balance. Employees are encouraged to take breaks, recharge, and care for themselves to perform at their best. People who use their strengths regularly tend to be more resilient and better able to cope with challenges and setbacks.

Innovation and creativity: By encouraging employees to use their strengths and take risks, a strengths-based culture can lead to greater innovation and creativity.

A strengths-based workplace culture can lead to a more engaged, productive, and positive work environment, ultimately contributing to the organization's success.

Creating a strengths-based workplace culture

Creating a strengths-based culture in the workplace requires intentional effort and commitment from leaders and managers. Here are some steps that organizations can take to create a strengths-based culture:

Define and communicate the organization's values: Develop a clear understanding of their values and how they align with a strengths-based culture. Then, communicate these values to employees and ensure they are reflected in the organization's operations.

Train managers and leaders: Train managers and leaders on the principles of a strengths-based culture, including how to identify and develop employee strengths, provide regular feedback, and create opportunities for collaboration and learning.

Conduct a strengths assessment: Conduct a strengths assessment to help employees identify their unique strengths and develop an awareness of their strengths and those of their colleagues.

Provide development opportunities: Offer training and development programs focused on developing employee strengths, allowing employees to apply their strengths in their work, and encouraging employees to collaborate to build on their strengths.

Foster collaboration: Foster collaboration among employees, encouraging them to share their strengths and work together to achieve shared goals. Consider forming teams based on complementary strengths rather than traditional roles and responsibilities.

Recognize and celebrate strengths: Regularly recognize and celebrate employees' strengths and achievements. Use strengths-based language in performance evaluations and reward systems.

Prioritise employee well-being: Ensure employees have access to resources and support to maintain their well-being, such as flexible work arrangements, mental health support, and wellness programs.

Include Strengths in your recruitment approach: Strengths-based hiring is an approach to recruitment and selection that focuses on identifying and leveraging job candidates' strengths. Instead of solely focusing on a candidate's qualifications, experience, and technical skills, strengths-based hiring considers their character strengths, personality traits, and other non-technical qualities.

Identifying character strengths in job candidates

In a strengths-based hiring process, recruiters and hiring managers use a variety of tools and techniques to assess a candidate's strengths, such as:

Behavioural interviews: Ask candidates to describe specific instances in which they demonstrated a particular strength.

Psychometric assessments: Using standardized tests to measure a candidate's personality traits, such as emotional intelligence, resilience, and optimism.

Role plays or simulations: Having candidates participate in exercises that simulate real-life work situations, such as problem-solving exercises, team activities, or customer interactions.

Reference checks: Asking previous employers or colleagues to provide insights into a candidate's strengths, work style, and interpersonal skills.

The aim of strengths-based hiring is to identify candidates with the necessary technical skills and qualifications and possess the character strengths and personal qualities that align with the organization's values and culture. This approach can help organizations build a more engaged, productive, and high-performing workforce.

Creating a strengths-based culture requires a holistic approach involving all levels of the organization, from leadership to frontline employees. Organizations can build a more engaged, productive, and positive work environment by prioritizing, developing, and using employee strengths.

Leadership in a strengths-based culture

Leadership plays a crucial role in building and sustaining a strengths-based workplace culture. Here are some key ways in which leaders can contribute to a strengths-based workplace culture:

Lead by example: Leaders should model the behaviour they want to see in their employees, focusing on strengths and positive reinforcement.

Communicate the importance of strengths: You should clearly communicate to employees the importance of developing and utilizing their strengths and how they contribute to the organization's success.

Provide training and resources: They should provide training and resources to help employees identify their strengths, develop new skills, and use their strengths to achieve their goals.

Foster a collaborative culture: We should create a culture that values collaboration, teamwork, and building on each other's strengths.

Recognize and celebrate strengths: Managers should regularly recognize and celebrate employees' strengths and achievements, using strengths-based language in performance evaluations and reward systems.

Prioritise employee well-being: Departments should prioritize employee well-being, recognizing that employees who feel supported and valued are more likely to use their strengths and contribute to the organization's success.

Monitor and adjust the culture: Organisational development specialists should monitor the organization's culture and adjust as needed to remain focused on strengths and positive reinforcement.

Leadership plays a critical role in creating and maintaining a strengths-based workplace culture. By leading by example, communicating the importance of strengths, providing training and resources, fostering collaboration, recognizing strengths, prioritizing employee well-being, and monitoring and adjusting the culture, leaders can build a positive and productive work environment that values and utilizes employee strengths.

You take your character with you

We invest much time and effort in training potential staff for international postings if we are a global organization. The one trait you take with you and is a crucial determinant of success is your character – people will see your Values In Action.

Working in a foreign culture can present unique challenges and opportunities. Therefore, several character strengths can be beneficial in such a situation. Here are some of the character strengths that can be most applicable to working in a foreign culture:

Cultural Competence - This character strength involves being aware of and respectful towards different cultures and adapting to the customs and practices of the local culture. Cultural competence is critical for building positive relationships with local colleagues and clients in a foreign culture. This can include understanding social norms, taboos, and etiquette, as well as being aware of the historical and political context of the culture. Having cultural competence also means adapting your communication style to suit the local culture, such as using appropriate forms of address and showing appropriate deference and respect.

Open-Mindedness involves being receptive to new ideas and perspectives and willing to challenge one's assumptions. In a foreign culture, open-mindedness is essential for navigating differences in communication styles, attitudes, and beliefs. It requires being open to different ways of thinking and seeing things differently. Being open-minded also means being willing to learn from local colleagues and clients and adapting your approach and strategies to suit the local context.

Adaptability - This trait involves being flexible and adjusting to changing circumstances. In a foreign culture, adaptability is critical for coping with the challenges of working in a different environment. This can include dealing with language barriers, cultural norms, and unexpected situations. It also requires being able to adjust to different work styles and schedules and being able to adapt to different expectations and standards.

Empathy - This dimension involves understanding and relating to the feelings and perspectives of others. In a foreign culture, empathy is vital for building trust and rapport with local colleagues and clients. It requires being able to understand the local culture and social norms and being able to adjust your behaviour accordingly. It also requires listening actively and showing a genuine interest in the concerns and needs of others.

Resilience - This attribute involves bouncing back from setbacks and challenges. In a foreign culture, resilience is essential for coping with the stresses of adjusting to a new environment. This can include dealing with culture shock, language barriers, and other challenges. It requires staying positive and maintaining a sense of perspective, even in difficult circumstances. It also requires drawing on your strengths and resources to overcome obstacles and achieve your goals.

Patience - This strength involves tolerating delays, difficulties, and frustrations without becoming overly anxious or upset. In a foreign culture, patience is essential for navigating differences in communication styles, cultural norms, and bureaucratic processes. It requires staying calm and focused in the face of uncertainty and ambiguity. It also requires maintaining a sense of humour and perspective, even when things don't go according to plan.

These six character strengths are critical for success in a foreign culture. By developing these strengths, you can build strong relationships with local colleagues and clients, navigate cultural differences and challenges, and achieve your goals in a new and unfamiliar environment.

Chapter 8: Leveraging Strengths for Teamwork

Teamwork, talents, and character strengths are closely intertwined in the workplace. When employees work together in teams, they often can leverage each other's unique strengths to achieve shared goals.

As I have written in 'Create a Resilient Project Management and Delivery Culture', creating a healthy team climate requires deliberate efforts by team leaders and members to foster an environment where everyone feels valued, respected, and supported. Building trust is essential for creating a healthy team climate. Encourage open communication, support team members, and lead by example to foster a culture of trust.

Encourage team members to build positive relationships with one another. This can be done through team-building activities or social events that allow team members to connect and build relationships. Establish expectations for how team members should work together. This practice can include guidelines for communication, collaboration, and conflict resolution.

Foster a collaborative environment where team members work together to achieve shared goals. Encourage team members to share their ideas and expertise to find the best solutions. Recognize and celebrate achievements by team members. This recognition can be done through public recognition, rewards, or other forms of appreciation.

Encourage team members to provide feedback to one another. This can be done through regular performance reviews or anonymous feedback channels. Provide opportunities for team members to develop their skills and knowledge. These opportunities can include training, mentorship, or other forms of professional development.

Address conflicts as soon as they arise. Encourage team members to work together to find a constructive and respectful solution. Encourage team members to achieve a healthy work-life balance. This can be done by offering flexible working arrangements or resources to help team members manage their workload.

How teamwork and strengths are related:

Complementary strengths: When employees work in teams, they often have complementary strengths that can be used to achieve shared goals. For example, one team member may have a strength in creativity. In contrast, another team member may have a strength in planning and organizing.

Teams with various strengths are often better at problem-solving. They can approach challenges from different angles and perspectives. By working together and leveraging their collective strengths, they can develop innovative solutions to complex problems.

Collaboration: Teamwork requires collaboration, which involves communication, trust, and mutual respect. When team members understand and appreciate each other's strengths, they are more likely to collaborate effectively, with each member contributing their unique strengths to the team.

By utilizing character strengths, team members can better understand each other's preferences and how they can contribute to the team's success. This approach improves collaboration and enables team members to work together more effectively towards achieving shared goals.

Positive reinforcement: Teams that focus on strengths are more likely to provide positive reinforcement to team members, which can improve team morale and productivity. By recognizing and celebrating each other's strengths, team members are more likely to feel valued and motivated.

Increased job satisfaction: Team members feel more engaged and fulfilled. When team members can use their strengths to contribute to their success, they are likelier to feel a sense of purpose and satisfaction in their work.

Overall, teamwork and character strengths are closely intertwined in the workplace. By leveraging each other's strengths and collaborating effectively, teams can achieve shared goals, improve problem-solving, and enhance team performance.

Individual strengths in a team

Identifying individuals' character strengths in a team will improve team performance and productivity. Here are some steps you can take to identify and leverage character strengths in a team:

Conduct a strengths assessment: Start by having each team member complete a strengths assessment, such as the VIA Character Strengths Survey. This will help you identify each team member's top strengths and how they can be leveraged.

Share strengths profiles: Once each team member has completed a strengths assessment, share the results with the team. This will help team members better understand each other's strengths and how they can be leveraged to achieve team goals.

Assign tasks based on strengths: Assign tasks and responsibilities to team members based on their strengths. For example, if one team member has a creativity strength, assign tasks that require creative thinking. If another team member has a leadership strength, assign tasks that involve leading and motivating the team.

Encourage strengths-based feedback: Encourage team members to provide feedback to each other based on their strengths. For example, if one team member demonstrates strength in teamwork, provide positive feedback highlighting that strength.

Provide opportunities for growth and development: For team members to develop their strengths further. This may include providing training and development opportunities or assigning tasks that challenge them to use their strengths in new ways.

Celebrate strengths-based achievements: Celebrate achievements that are based on individual strengths. This will help reinforce the importance of leveraging strengths in the team and motivate team members to continue using their strengths to achieve team goals.

Identifying and leveraging individual character strengths in a team can help improve team performance and productivity. By conducting a strengths assessment, sharing strengths profiles, assigning tasks based on strengths, encouraging strengths-based feedback, providing opportunities for growth and development, and celebrating strengths-based achievements, you can create a strengths-based team culture that promotes collaboration and enhances overall team performance.

Building a strengths-based team culture

Building a strengths-based team culture involves creating an environment that values and leverages individual character strengths to achieve team goals. Here are some steps you can take to build a strengths-based team culture:

Educate the team: Educate the team on the importance of character strengths and how they can be leveraged to achieve team goals. This will help team members understand the value of focusing on strengths and encourage them to recognize and leverage each other's strengths.

Conduct a team strengths assessment: Conduct a team strengths assessment to identify the team's collective strengths. This will help you understand the team's strengths and how they can be leveraged to achieve team goals.

Focus on strengths in team meetings: Focus on strengths by highlighting individual strengths and discussing how they can be used to achieve team goals. Encourage team members to share examples of how they have leveraged their strengths to achieve success.

Assign tasks based on strengths: Assign tasks and responsibilities based on individual strengths. This will help team members use their strengths to contribute to the team's success.

Encourage strengths-based feedback: Encourage team members to provide feedback to each other based on their strengths. This will help team members recognize and appreciate each other's strengths and reinforce the importance of leveraging strengths.

Provide opportunities for growth and development: For team members to develop their strengths further. This may include providing training and development opportunities or assigning tasks that challenge them to use their strengths in new ways.

Celebrate strengths-based achievements: Celebrate achievements based on individual and team strengths. This will help reinforce the importance of leveraging strengths in the team and motivate team members to continue using their strengths to achieve team goals.

Building a strengths-based team culture involves creating an environment that values and leverages individual character strengths to achieve team goals. By educating the team, conducting a team strengths assessment, focusing on strengths in team meetings, assigning tasks based on strengths, encouraging strengths-based feedback, providing opportunities for growth and development, and celebrating strengths-based achievements, you can create a strengths-based team culture that promotes collaboration and enhances overall team performance.

Overall, leveraging character strengths for teamwork can benefit both the team and individual team members. By understanding each other's strengths and how they can be used to achieve team goals, team members can work together more effectively, perform at a higher level, and feel more engaged and fulfilled in their work.

Coaching for motivation and improvement

If someone lacks hope or motivation, coaching them using their character strengths can be an effective way to help them tap into their internal resources and find the inspiration they need to move forward. Here are some steps you could take:

Identify the person's character strengths: The first step in using character strengths to coach someone lacking hope or motivation is to help them identify their own character strengths. Then, you can use a character strengths assessment tool like the VIA Survey, free and widely available online, to help them discover their top strengths.

Connect their strengths to their goals: Once you have identified their strengths, work with the person to identify their goals and aspirations. Then, help them see how their strengths can support and enhance their pursuit of those goals. For example, suppose their top strengths are creativity and curiosity. In that case, you might help them see how those strengths can be used to generate new ideas or find new solutions to challenges they may be facing.

Explore their values and passions: Often, a lack of hope or motivation can indicate a person feeling disconnected from their values and passions. By exploring what matters most to them, you can help them tap into their most profound sources of inspiration and motivation.

Set small, achievable goals: Sometimes, people lacking hope or motivation can become overwhelmed by the prospect of achieving large or complex goals. By breaking down their goals into small, achievable steps, you can help them build momentum and gain confidence in their ability to succeed.

Celebrate progress and successes: As the person progresses towards their goals, celebrate their successes, and acknowledge the positive impact of their character strengths. This can help build confidence and motivation and reinforce the connection between their strengths and their ability to achieve their goals.

Overall, using character strengths to coach someone lacking hope or motivation can be a powerful way to help them tap into their internal resources and find the inspiration they need to move forward. By helping them connect their strengths to their goals, explore their values and passions, set achievable goals, and celebrate their progress, you can help them build momentum and achieve success.

Chapter 9: Harnessing and Developing Character Strengths

Think of your strengths using the obvious metaphor, which comes to mind of a muscle in the body which supports you and enables you to move while keeping your balance, sometimes carrying a bigger load than normal but strong enough to bounce back.

Once you have developed your list of signature strengths and other strengths that you would like to develop as a priority, you will seek guidance on how to exercise or stretch that muscle.

Appreciation of Beauty and Excellence

Appreciation of Beauty and Excellence refers to the ability to find beauty, excellence, and meaning in everyday experiences, art, nature, and other sources of inspiration. Here are some tips for developing this strength:

Cultivate mindfulness: Pay attention to your surroundings and try to find beauty and excellence in the things around you. Notice the details, textures, colours, and sounds of the world.

Practice gratitude: Focus on what you are grateful for, including the beauty and excellence you encounter. Express your appreciation for these things to others.

Expose yourself to new experiences: Seek out new experiences and environments that expose you to new sources of beauty and excellence. For example, visit museums, concerts or plays, or hike in nature.

Learn about the arts: Educate yourself about the arts, whether it's visual art, music, literature, or another form. Take a class, read a book, or listen to a podcast to learn more about the art forms that interest you.

Practice creativity: Engage in creative activities that allow you to express yourself and explore beauty and excellence in new ways. This could be anything from painting to cooking to writing.

Practice positive thinking: Look for the positive aspects of situations and try to find beauty and excellence even in challenging circumstances. This can help you develop a more optimistic and appreciative outlook on life.

Developing the strength of appreciation of beauty and excellence is an ongoing process that requires practice, curiosity, and an open mind. However, it can be a rewarding journey to help you find more joy, meaning, and inspiration.

Bravery

Bravery is the ability to confront fear, pain, danger, or uncertainty confidently and firmly. Here are some tips to help you develop this strength:

Take small risks: Start by taking small risks that challenge you in a safe and controlled way. This can help you build confidence and develop your courage over time.

Face your fears: Identify the things that make you feel afraid and actively work to confront them. This can help you to overcome your fears and develop greater resilience.

Practice self-compassion: Be kind and compassionate towards yourself, especially when you face challenges or setbacks. This can help you to build inner strength and resilience in the face of adversity.

Surround yourself with supportive people: Seek out people who support and encourage you. This can help you to feel more confident and motivated to take on new challenges.

Stay motivated: Focus on your goals and stay motivated even in the face of obstacles. This can help you to push through difficult times and achieve your desired outcomes.

Learn from failure: Embrace failure as an opportunity to learn and grow. Recognize that failure is a natural part of the learning process and use it as a stepping stone to success.

Citizenship

Citizenship refers to the sense of responsibility and commitment to positively contributing to society. Here are some tips for developing this strength:

Get involved: Find ways to get involved in your community, whether volunteering, participating in local events, or joining community organizations. Look for opportunities to contribute your time and skills in meaningful ways.

Take action: Don't just talk about making a difference; take action. Identify issues or causes that are important to you and take steps to address them. This could include advocating for policy changes, organizing events or initiatives, or donating to a charity.

Develop empathy: Empathy is an essential component of citizenship. Develop your ability to understand and connect with others by practising active listening, seeking out diverse perspectives, and being open-minded.

Be a responsible citizen: Take responsibility for your actions and be accountable for their impact on others and the environment. This could include reducing your environmental footprint, supporting ethical and socially responsible businesses, or advocating for social justice.

Stay informed about local, national, and global issues and understand their impact on society. Keep updated with the news, research issues that interest you, and engage in critical thinking.

Educate others: Share your knowledge and skills with others to help them become more engaged and informed citizens. This could include teaching others about issues that are important to you, sharing resources, or mentoring others.

Creativity

Creativity refers to thinking outside the box, generating novel ideas, and approaching situations with originality and innovation. Here are some tips to help you develop this strength:

Practice brainstorming: Dedicate time to generate as many ideas as possible without judging their quality. This helps to stimulate your creativity and trains your brain to think differently.

Take breaks and engage in activities that you enjoy: Doing something that relaxes you or that you enjoy, such as listening to music, taking a walk in nature, or practising a hobby, can help you clear your mind and boost your creativity.

Challenge yourself: Try new things and take risks. Step out of your comfort zone and push yourself to explore different perspectives and approaches to problems.

Observe and learn: Pay attention to the world around you, observe people and their behaviours, and explore new places and experiences. This can help you to generate new ideas and insights.

Keep a journal: Writing down your ideas and thoughts can help you to reflect on your experiences and generate new insights. You can also use your journal to track your progress and set new goals.

Collaborate with others: Working with other people can help to stimulate your creativity by exposing you to new perspectives and ideas. Seek out opportunities to collaborate with others and exchange ideas.

Remember that creativity is a skill that can be developed and improved with practice. Therefore, incorporating these tips into your daily routine can enhance your VIA Strength of Creativity and bring more innovation and originality to your life.

Curiosity

Curiosity refers to the desire to learn new things and explore the world around you. Here are some tips to help you develop this strength:

Ask questions: Start by asking more questions, especially about things you don't know much about. This can help you to gain a better understanding of the world around you and stimulate your curiosity.

Explore new things: Try things you've never done before, such as travelling to new places, trying new foods, or learning a new language. This can help you to expand your knowledge and experience new things.

Read and watch documentaries: Read books, watch documentaries, and explore different sources of information. This can help you to learn new things and expand your knowledge base.

Surround yourself with curious people: Spend time with people who are curious about learning new things. Their energy can be contagious and help to stimulate your own curiosity.

Embrace the unknown: Be willing to embrace the unknown and take risks. This can help you to step out of your comfort zone and explore new experiences and opportunities.

Practice mindfulness: Cultivate a sense of curiosity and wonder about the present moment. Pay attention to the details of your surroundings, notice things you might have missed before, and explore the world with a fresh perspective.

Fairness

Fairness refers to the ability to treat all people equally and without bias. Here are some tips to help you develop this strength:

Examine your biases: Reflect on your beliefs and biases and how they may affect your perceptions and interactions with others. This can help you identify areas where you may need to challenge your assumptions or prejudices.

Seek diverse perspectives: Make an effort to seek out diverse perspectives and opinions on important issues. This can help you to gain a deeper understanding of different perspectives and experiences.

Be open-minded: Consider new ideas and perspectives, even if they challenge your beliefs. This can help you to avoid becoming rigid in your thinking and more receptive to different viewpoints.

Advocate for others: Speak up and take action when you see unfair treatment or discrimination against others. This can help to create a more equitable and just society.

Be consistent: Treat all people fairly and consistently, regardless of their background, beliefs, or identity. This can help to build trust and respect with others.

Practice self-awareness: Be aware of your biases and how they may influence your perceptions and decisions. This can help you to recognize when you are being unfair or unjust and make changes to address these issues.

Incorporating these tips into your daily routine can enhance your Strength of Fairness.

Forgiveness

Forgiveness refers to letting go of resentment and anger towards someone who has wronged you. Here are some tips for developing this strength:

Practice empathy: Try to see the situation from the other person's perspective. This can help you understand their motivations and make it easier to forgive them.

Focus on the present: Let go of the past and focus on the present moment. Dwelling on past hurts can keep you in a negative cycle and prevent you from moving forward.

Cultivate compassion: Cultivate compassion for yourself and others. Recognize that everyone makes mistakes and that forgiving someone can help you progress.

Practice mindfulness: Mindfulness can help you stay present and focused, making letting go of negative emotions easier. Try meditating, practising deep breathing, or engaging in other mindfulness practices.

Set boundaries: Forgiveness does not mean that you have to tolerate toxic or abusive behaviour. Set healthy boundaries for yourself and communicate them clearly to others.

Seek support: Forgiveness can be a difficult process, and it can be helpful to seek support from friends, family, or a therapist.

Remember that developing the strength of forgiveness is an ongoing process that requires practice, patience, and self-compassion. It can be a challenging journey, but the rewards of letting go of resentment and anger can be life-changing.

Gratitude

Gratitude refers to the ability to feel and express thankfulness and appreciation for the good things in one's life, including other people, experiences, and possessions. Here are some tips for developing this strength:

Keep a gratitude journal: Daily, write down three things you are grateful for. This can help you focus on the positive aspects of your life and cultivate a sense of appreciation.

Express gratitude: Take the time to thank others for their kindness, support, or help. Letting others know you appreciate them can strengthen your relationships and enhance your connection.

Practice mindfulness: Pay attention to the present moment and notice the small things you might normally overlook. Cultivate a sense of awe and wonder for the beauty and goodness in the world.

Focus on what you have, not what you lack: Instead of dwelling on what you don't have, focus on the blessings in your life. Recognize that even the small things can bring joy and gratitude.

Volunteer or give back: Giving to others can increase your sense of gratitude and well-being. Look for ways to volunteer in your community or donate to a charity that aligns with your values.

Practice self-compassion: Be kind and gentle with yourself, especially during challenging times. Recognize that it's okay to struggle and make mistakes, and focus on what you are doing well.

Remember that developing the strength of gratitude is an ongoing process that requires practice, intention, and mindfulness.

Honesty

Honesty refers to being truthful and transparent in your words and actions. Here are some tips to help you develop this strength:

Practice self-awareness: Be aware of your thoughts, feelings, and motivations. This can help you identify when you may be tempted to stretch or hide the truth.

Set ethical standards: Develop a clear sense of your ethical standards and hold yourself accountable. This can help you to stay true to your values and make honest decisions.

Be open and transparent in your communication, and avoid withholding information or misrepresenting the truth. This can help you to build trust and credibility with others.

Practice active listening: Listen actively and attentively to others, and respond honestly and authentically. This can help you to build stronger relationships based on trust and respect.

Accept responsibility: Take responsibility for your actions and decisions, and be willing to admit when you have made a mistake or acted dishonestly. This can help you to learn from your mistakes and grow as a person.

Seek feedback: Seek feedback from others on your communication style and behaviours, and be open to constructive criticism. This can help you identify improvement areas and work towards becoming a more honest and authentic person.

Incorporating these tips into your daily routine can enhance your VIA Strength of Honesty and bring more authenticity and trustworthiness to your interactions with others.

Hope

Hope refers to the ability to maintain a positive outlook and a sense of confidence in the future, even in the face of challenges or adversity. Here are some tips for developing this strength:

Set realistic goals: Identify challenging but achievable goals, and work towards them systematically. A sense of purpose and direction can increase your hope and optimism.

Focus on solutions: Instead of dwelling on problems, focus on finding solutions. This can help you feel more in control of your situation and increase your sense of hopefulness.

Practice self-compassion: Be kind and understanding towards yourself, especially during difficult times. Remember that setbacks and failures are a normal part of the journey, and focus on what you can learn from them.

Seek support: Reach out to friends, family, or a mental health professional if you struggle to maintain hope or optimism. Remember that seeking help is a sign of strength, not weakness.

Reframe negative thoughts: Challenge negative thoughts and beliefs that may be limiting your sense of hope. Instead, focus on positive outcomes and possibilities, and look for evidence that supports a more hopeful outlook.

Cultivate gratitude: Focus on the good things in your life and express gratitude for them. This can help you maintain a more positive and hopeful perspective, even during difficult times.

It can be a powerful tool for increasing your overall well-being and helping you navigate life's challenges more confidently and optimistically.

Humility

Humility refers to the ability to recognize and appreciate one's own limitations and to have a modest and humble view of oneself. Here are some tips for developing this strength:

Practice self-reflection: Take time to reflect on your own thoughts, feelings, and actions. Reflect on your strengths, weaknesses, and areas for growth. This can help you develop a more realistic and humble view of yourself.

Listen to others: Practice active listening and be open to feedback from others. Be willing to learn from others and consider their perspectives and insights.

Practice gratitude: Focus on the things you are grateful for in your life. Recognize the contributions of others and express your appreciation for their efforts.

Be willing to learn: Adopt a growth mindset and be willing to learn from your mistakes. Recognize that you don't have all the answers and that there is always room for growth and improvement.

Serve others: Practice acts of kindness and service towards others. This can help you develop greater empathy and compassion towards others and a more humble view of yourself.

Practice mindfulness: Mindfulness can help you stay present and focused, making it easier to stay grounded and humble. Try meditating, practising deep breathing, or engaging in other mindfulness practices.

It can be challenging, but the rewards of developing a more humble view of oneself can be profound.

Humour

Humour refers to finding the humorous aspects of life, situations, and oneself. Here are some tips for developing this strength:

Practice playful curiosity: Cultivate a sense of curiosity and playfulness about the world around you. Look for the absurd, the unexpected, or the quirky aspects of life and situations.

Find joy in the everyday: Look for the small moments of joy and humour in your daily life, whether it's a funny conversation with a friend, a silly joke, or a playful activity.

Laugh at yourself: Learn to laugh at your own mistakes, quirks, and imperfections. This can help you develop a more lighthearted and accepting attitude towards yourself.

Seek out humour: Watch a funny movie, read a humorous book, or attend a comedy show. Surround yourself with people who have a good sense of humour and who make you laugh.

Use humour to cope: Use humour as a coping mechanism during challenging times. It can help you reframe a situation, reduce stress, and find a new perspective.

Practice kindness: Use humour to connect with others and bring joy to their lives. Share a funny story, make a joke, or find a way to lighten the mood.

Kindness

Kindness refers to the ability to be compassionate, caring, and empathetic towards others. Here are some tips to help you develop this strength:

Practice empathy: Put yourself in other people's shoes, and try to understand their perspective and feelings. This can help you to develop greater compassion and empathy towards others.

Be attentive and present: Pay attention to others when they speak, and be fully present in your interactions with them. This can help show that you care and are interested in their well-being.

Show appreciation: Express gratitude and appreciation towards others for their kindness, support, or contributions. This can help to strengthen your relationships and foster a sense of goodwill.

Offer help: Look for opportunities to offer help or support to others, whether through a kind word, a small gesture, or a more significant act of kindness. This can help to demonstrate your compassion and care for others.

Practice forgiveness: Forgive others and yourself for past mistakes or misunderstandings. This can help to cultivate a more compassionate and empathetic attitude towards others.

Be respectful: Treat others with respect and dignity, regardless of their background or circumstances. This can help to create a more inclusive and supportive environment for everyone.

Incorporating these tips into your daily routine can enhance your Strength of Kindness and bring more compassion, care, and empathy to your interactions with others.

Leadership

Leadership refers to inspiring and guiding others towards a shared vision or goal. Here are some tips for developing this strength:

Lead by example: Model the behaviour you expect from others. Be a positive role model and demonstrate the values and behaviours that you want your team to embody.

Communicate effectively: Communication is a key component of effective leadership. Practice active listening, be clear and concise in your messaging, and tailor your communication style to the needs of your team.

Develop a vision: Strong leaders clearly know where they want their team to go. Develop a compelling vision and communicate it to your team in a way that inspires and motivates them.

Build relationships: Build strong relationships with your team members based on trust, respect, and open communication. Take the time to get to know your team members individually and understand their strengths and challenges.

Develop your emotional intelligence: Emotional intelligence is essential for effective leadership. Develop self-awareness, empathy, and social skills to better understand and connect with your team members.

Delegate effectively: Delegation is a key leadership skill. Delegate tasks and responsibilities to team members based on their strengths and development needs and provide the support and resources they need to succeed.

Continuously learn and grow: Seek feedback, learn from your successes and failures, and invest in your personal and professional development.

Love

Love refers to expressing and receiving love in healthy and meaningful ways. Here are some tips to help you develop this strength:

Cultivate self-love: Learn to love, accept yourself unconditionally, and treat yourself with compassion, kindness, and respect. This can help you to develop a more positive and healthy relationship with yourself.

Practice gratitude: Focus on the positive aspects of your life and express gratitude for them, including the people you love and who love you. This can help you to develop a greater appreciation for the love in your life.

Nurture your relationships: Make time to connect with those you love and care about, and prioritize your relationships with them. This can help deepen your connections and show your love in meaningful ways.

Communicate openly and honestly: Be open and honest in communicating with the people you love, and express your thoughts, feelings, and needs clearly and respectfully. This can help to build trust and strengthen your relationships.

Practice empathy: Try to understand and empathize with the feelings and perspectives of the people you love, even when disagreeing. This can help to foster greater understanding and compassion in your relationships.

Show affection and appreciation: Express your love through physical touch, kind words, and small gestures of affection and appreciation. This can help to reinforce the love and connection between you and the people you care about.

Love of Learning

Love of Learning refers to a deep and abiding passion for learning, acquiring new knowledge, and engaging with the world around you. Here are some tips to help you develop this strength:

Set learning goals: Identify specific topics or areas you want to learn more about and set goals for yourself. This can help you to stay motivated and focused on your learning journey.

Read widely: Read books, articles, and other sources of information on various topics, both inside and outside your field of expertise. This can help broaden your knowledge and deepen your understanding of the world.

Seek out learning opportunities: Look for opportunities to attend workshops, conferences, and other events that align with your interests and goals. This can help you to connect with like-minded people and gain new insights and perspectives.

Embrace challenges: Embrace them as opportunities to learn and grow. Approach difficult tasks with a positive attitude and a willingness to learn from mistakes.

Experiment and explore: Experiment with different approaches to learning and explore different learning methods, such as online courses, podcasts, or learning apps. This can help you find the best methods and keep your learning journey interesting and engaging.

Share your knowledge: Share your knowledge and expertise with others. Teaching others can help to deepen your own understanding of a subject and provide you with new insights and perspectives.

Open-mindedness

Open-mindedness is the ability to consider new ideas and perspectives with an open and non-judgmental mindset. Here are some tips to help you develop this strength:

Practice active listening: When someone expresses their views, consciously listen to what they are saying without interrupting or judging. This can help you better understand their perspective and broaden your thinking.

Seek out diverse viewpoints: Read or watch news sources that present differing viewpoints, and seek out conversations with people who have different opinions or life experiences from your own. This can help you to develop a more nuanced understanding of the world.

Challenge your own assumptions: Recognize and challenge your own biases and preconceptions. Consider how your experiences and beliefs may influence your thinking. Be open to changing your mind if presented with new information.

Practice empathy: Try to see things from the perspective of others and understand their emotions and experiences. This can help you to develop a more compassionate and open-minded attitude towards others.

Embrace uncertainty: Accept that there are often multiple ways to interpret a situation and that not everything is black and white. Therefore, be open to ambiguity and uncertainty, and seek to understand the complexity of different viewpoints.

Learn from mistakes: Be open to learning from your own mistakes and failures and those of others. Recognize that mistakes and failures can provide valuable learning opportunities and help you to grow and develop your thinking.

Perspective

Perspective refers to the ability to see things from multiple angles, understand different viewpoints, and recognize the complexity of situations. Here are some tips to help you develop this strength:

Practice empathy: Empathy is the ability to understand and share the feelings of others. When you practice empathy, you can better see things from someone else's perspective, which can help you develop your own perspective.

Challenge your assumptions: Recognize and challenge your own biases and preconceptions. Consider how your experiences and beliefs may influence your thinking. Be open to changing your mind if presented with new information.

Seek out diverse viewpoints: Seek out conversations with people who have different opinions or life experiences from your own. This can help you to broaden your understanding of the world and develop a more nuanced perspective.

Read widely: Read books, articles, and other sources of information on various topics, both inside and outside your field of expertise. This can help you to deepen your knowledge and gain a more comprehensive understanding of the world.

Travel and explore new cultures: Travel to new places and immerse yourself in different cultures. This can help you to broaden your perspective and gain a deeper understanding of different ways of living and thinking.

Practice mindfulness: Cultivate awareness and curiosity about the present moment. Pay attention to the details of your surroundings, notice things you might have missed before, and explore the world with a fresh perspective.

Perseverance

Perseverance refers to the ability to persist in facing obstacles, setbacks, and challenges. Here are some tips to help you develop this strength:

Set achievable goals: Set clear and achievable goals for yourself, and break them down into smaller steps. This can help you to stay motivated and focused on your progress.

Develop a growth mindset: Adopt a growth mindset, and recognize that challenges and setbacks are opportunities to learn and grow. Focus on the process of learning and improvement rather than just the end result.

Practice self-discipline: Develop a habit of self-discipline by setting routines, prioritizing your time, and avoiding distractions. This can help you to stay focused and on track towards your goals.

Stay positive: Focus on the positive aspects of your journey, and practice gratitude for your progress so far. This can help you to stay motivated and overcome negative self-talk.

Seek support: Seek out the support of friends, family, or a mentor when facing challenges or setbacks. Having a supportive network can provide motivation, encouragement, and accountability.

Embrace failure: Embrace failure as a natural part of the learning process. Use it as an opportunity to learn and grow. Celebrate your successes and learn from your mistakes.

Prudence

Prudence refers to the ability to think carefully and make wise decisions based on sound judgement and practical wisdom. Here are some tips for developing this strength:

Cultivate self-awareness: Reflect on your values, beliefs, and goals. This can help you make decisions aligned with your values and priorities.

Practice critical thinking: Learn to evaluate information critically and make informed decisions based on evidence and logic. This can help you avoid making impulsive decisions or being swayed by emotions.

Consider the consequences: Consider the consequences of your actions and decisions. Consider both the short-term and long-term impacts on yourself and others.

Seek advice: Seek advice and guidance from others, especially those with more experience or expertise. Be open to feedback and different perspectives.

Learn from mistakes: Learn from your mistakes and use them as opportunities for growth and learning. Reflect on what went wrong and how you can do better next time.

Practice patience: Take time to think through decisions and avoid rushing into them. Be patient and willing to gather more information if needed.

Remember that developing the strength of prudence is an ongoing process that requires practice, self-reflection, and a willingness to learn and grow. It can be a challenging journey, but the rewards of making wise and thoughtful decisions can be significant.

Self-Regulation

Self-Regulation refers to the ability to manage one's emotions, impulses, and behaviours in a way that is appropriate for the situation. Here are some tips for developing this strength:

Practice mindfulness: Mindfulness can help you become more aware of your thoughts, feelings, and bodily sensations, which can help you regulate your emotions and impulses more effectively. Try meditating, practising deep breathing, or engaging in other mindfulness practices.

Develop healthy habits: Establish healthy habits, such as getting enough sleep, eating a balanced diet, and exercising regularly. These habits can help you regulate your emotions and behaviours more effectively.

Identify triggers: Learn to identify the situations or people that tend to trigger your negative emotions or impulses. Once you can identify these triggers, you can develop strategies to manage them more effectively.

Practice relaxation techniques: Learn and practice relaxation techniques, such as progressive muscle relaxation or guided imagery. These techniques can help you manage stress and regulate your emotions.

Set goals: Set realistic goals for yourself and work towards them systematically. This can help you stay focused and motivated and avoid impulsive behaviours or decisions.

Seek support: Seek support from friends, family, or a mental health professional if you struggle to manage your emotions or behaviours. Remember that seeking help is a sign of strength, not weakness.

Social Intelligence

Social Intelligence refers to the ability to understand and navigate social situations effectively. Here are some tips to help you develop this strength:

Practice active listening: Pay close attention to what others are saying and show that you are listening by asking questions and summarizing what they have said. This can help you to better understand their perspectives and feelings.

Observe body language and nonverbal cues: Be aware of the nonverbal cues that people use, such as facial expressions, tone of voice, and body language. This can help you to better understand their emotions and intentions.

Practice empathy: Try to understand and empathize with the feelings and perspectives of others, even if you disagree with them. This can help you to build stronger relationships and resolve conflicts more effectively.

Be adaptable: Be willing to adapt your behaviour and communication style to suit different social situations and personalities. This can help you to build rapport and establish trust with a wide range of people.

Build rapport: Look for common ground and shared interests when interacting with others. Use this to build rapport and establish connections. This can help you to establish stronger relationships and foster greater cooperation and collaboration.

Manage emotions: Be aware of your emotions and how they may impact your interactions with others. Practice emotional regulation techniques like deep breathing or mindfulness to manage your emotions effectively.

Spirituality

Spirituality refers to a sense of connection to something greater than oneself, such as a higher power, nature, or humanity. Here are some tips for developing this strength:

Explore your beliefs: Take the time to explore your beliefs about spirituality and what gives your life meaning. This can involve reading spiritual texts, attending religious services, or engaging in spiritual practices like meditation or prayer.

Cultivate mindfulness: Pay attention to the present moment and cultivate awareness and acceptance. This can help you connect with a greater sense of purpose and meaning in life.

Practice gratitude: Express gratitude for the things in your life that bring you joy and fulfilment. Recognize that these things are connected to something greater than yourself.

Connect with others: Seek opportunities to connect with others who share your spiritual beliefs, whether through religious services, spiritual retreats, or community events.

Engage in acts of service: Find ways to serve others and contribute to something greater than yourself. This can involve volunteering, donating to a charity, or simply being kind and compassionate towards others.

Find beauty in nature: Spend time in nature and appreciate the beauty and wonder of the natural world. This can help you connect with a greater sense of spirituality and awe.

Remember that developing the strength of spirituality is a personal journey that may look different for everyone. It involves connecting with something greater than oneself and finding meaning and purpose in life

Teamwork

Teamwork refers to the ability to work collaboratively with others to achieve a common goal. Here are some tips for developing this strength:

Develop effective communication skills: Effective communication is the foundation of teamwork. To improve your communication skills, practice active listening, ask for feedback, and work on delivering clear and concise messages.

Build trust: Trust is essential for successful teamwork. Be reliable, transparent, and supportive of your teammates. Establish open and honest communication channels and be accountable for your actions.

Foster a positive team culture: Create an environment encouraging teamwork, mutual respect, and constructive feedback. Celebrate team successes and learn from failures together.

Develop emotional intelligence: Emotional intelligence helps you understand and manage your emotions and those of others. It also helps you build strong relationships with your team members. Develop your emotional intelligence by practising self-awareness, empathy, and social skills.

Practice collaboration: Work on developing your collaborative skills by seeking opportunities to work on group projects, brainstorming sessions, or team-building activities. Practice active participation, compromise, and flexibility.

Seek out diverse perspectives: Embrace diversity and seek out perspectives that are different from your own. This can help you develop creative solutions to problems and build a more inclusive team culture.

Zest

Zest refers to the ability to approach life with energy, excitement, and enthusiasm. Here are some tips to help you develop this strength:

Set goals and challenge yourself: Identify new goals or challenges that excite you, and push yourself outside your comfort zone. This can help you to feel more energized and engaged with your life.

Practice mindfulness: Cultivate a sense of present-moment awareness, and focus on fully engaging in each moment with curiosity and enthusiasm.

Engage in physical activity: Regular physical activity, such as exercise or sports, can help boost energy levels and improve mood.

Surround yourself with positivity: Seek out positive people, media, and experiences that uplift and inspire you. This can help you to maintain a more positive outlook on life.

Take breaks: Make time for rest and relaxation, and enjoy leisure activities that bring you joy and rejuvenation.

Practice gratitude: Focus on the positive aspects of your life and express gratitude for them. This can help you to maintain a more optimistic outlook.

Incorporating these tips into your daily routine can enhance your Zest and bring more energy and enthusiasm to your life.

Conclusion:

The future of character strengths in the workplace is promising as more and more organizations recognize the value of a strengths-based approach to employee development and performance. Here are a few trends that are likely to shape the future of character strengths in the workplace:

Continued adoption of strengths-based approaches: As more organizations experience the benefits of a strengths-based approach, this approach will likely become more widespread. This may involve integrating strengths-based approaches into hiring, performance evaluations, and leadership development programs.

Greater emphasis on individualized development: As technology advances, we will likely see more individualized development programs tailored to each employee's unique strengths and needs. This may involve using data analytics and machine learning to identify areas where employees can improve and then creating customized development plans that leverage their unique strengths.

Increased use of technology: Technology is likely to play an increasingly important role in the future of character strengths in the workplace. This may involve using virtual reality simulations to help employees practice using their strengths in different scenarios or online platforms to facilitate strengths-based coaching and mentoring.

More focus on positive psychology: Positive psychology, which focuses on human behaviour's strengths and positive aspects, will likely become more prominent in the workplace. This may involve incorporating positive psychology principles into leadership development programs or using positive psychology

By focusing on the strengths of their employees and leaders, these organizations have created a culture of positivity, collaboration, and continuous improvement.

Conclusion:

The future of character strengths in the workplace is promising as more and more organizations recognize the value of a strengths-based approach to employee development and performance. Here are a few trends that are likely to shape the future of character strengths in the workplace:

Continued adoption of strengths-based approaches: As more organizations experience the benefits of a strengths-based approach, this approach will likely become more widespread. This may involve integrating strengths-based approaches into hiring, performance evaluations, and leadership development programs.

Greater emphasis on individualized development: As technology advances, we will likely see more individualized development programs tailored to each employee's unique strengths and needs. This may involve using data analytics and machine learning to identify areas where employees can improve and then creating customized development plans that leverage their unique strengths.

Increased use of technology: Technology is likely to play an increasingly important role in the future of character strengths in the workplace. This may involve using virtual reality simulations to help employees practice using their strengths in different scenarios or online platforms to facilitate strengths-based coaching and mentoring.

More focus on positive psychology: Positive psychology, which focuses on human behaviour's strengths and positive aspects, will likely become more prominent in the workplace. This may involve incorporating positive psychology principles into leadership development programs or using positive psychology interventions to improve employee well-being and performance.

Overall, the future of character strengths in the workplace is bright as more organizations recognize the value of a strengths-based approach to employee development and performance. By leveraging their employees' unique strengths, organizations can create a culture of positivity, collaboration, and continuous improvement that drives success and innovation.

Appendix

The Psychiatric Diagnostic Handbook is a reference book that provides a comprehensive guide to diagnosing and classifying mental disorders. The handbook describes each mental disorder, including symptoms, prevalence, risk factors, and treatment options.

The Psychiatric Diagnostic Handbook is used by mental health professionals, including psychiatrists, psychologists, and clinical social workers, to assist in diagnosing and treating mental disorders. The handbook is organized according to the Diagnostic and Statistical Manual of Mental Disorders (DSM), published by the American Psychiatric Association and considered the standard reference for mental health diagnoses in the United States.

The DSM provides a set of diagnostic criteria for each mental disorder, used to identify and classify mental disorders based on the presence and severity of specific symptoms. The criteria are based on extensive research and are periodically revised to reflect new scientific knowledge and changes in clinical practice.

The Psychiatric Diagnostic Handbook is an important resource for mental health professionals, providing a standard approach to diagnosing and classifying mental disorders. By using the handbook, mental health professionals can ensure that their diagnoses are accurate and consistent and can provide appropriate treatment and support to individuals with mental health conditions.)

By focusing on the strengths of their employees and leaders, these organizations have created a culture of positivity, collaboration, and continuous improvement.

Organizations using strengths for success

Several examples of organizations have successfully implemented a strengths-based approach to achieve greater success. Here are a few examples:

Microsoft: Microsoft has integrated a strengths-based approach into its performance management system, which has led to improved employee engagement and satisfaction. The company uses the Gallup StrengthsFinder assessment to help employees identify their strengths and then encourages managers to leverage those strengths in their employees' work.

PepsiCo: PepsiCo has incorporated a strengths-based approach into its leadership development programs. The company uses a 360-degree feedback tool to help leaders identify their strengths and then works with them to build on those strengths to improve their performance.

Deloitte: Deloitte has implemented a strengths-based approach in its talent development programs, which has resulted in increased employee engagement and retention. The company uses the Clifton StrengthsFinder assessment to help employees identify their strengths and then works with them to integrate those strengths into their work.

Sanofi: Sanofi, a global pharmaceutical company, has used a strengths-based approach to improve employee engagement and performance. The company uses a strengths-based leadership program to help managers identify and leverage their and their team member's strengths to achieve greater success.

These examples demonstrate how organizations can use a strengths-based approach to improve employee engagement, performance, and retention and achieve greater success overall.

Printed in Great Britain
by Amazon